THE HUMAN BEHIND THE HERO
CHADWICK BOSEMAN IS BLACK PANTHER®

HOT TOPICS

BY KATIE KAWA

Gareth Stevens
PUBLISHING

Please visit our website, www.garethstevens.com. For a free color catalog of all our high-quality books, call toll free 1-800-542-2595 or fax 1-877-542-2596.

Library of Congress Cataloging-in-Publication Data

Names: Kawa, Katie, author.
Title: Chadwick Boseman is Black Panther / Katie Kawa.
Description: New York : Gareth Stevens Publishing, [2020] | Series: The human behind the hero | Includes index.
Identifiers: LCCN 2019012184| ISBN 9781538248232 (pbk.) | ISBN 9781538248256 (library bound) | ISBN 9781538248249 (6 pack)
Subjects: LCSH: Boseman, Chadwick–Juvenile literature. | African American entertainers–Biography–Juvenile literature.
Classification: LCC PN2287.B645 K39 2020 | DDC 791.4302/8092 [B] –dc23
LC record available at https://lccn.loc.gov/2019012184

First Edition

Published in 2020 by
Gareth Stevens Publishing
111 East 14th Street, Suite 349
New York, NY 10003

Designer: Sarah Liddell
Editor: Katie Kawa

Photo credits: Cover, p. 1 Tinseltown/Shutterstock.com; halftone texture used throughout gn8/Shutterstock.com; comic frame used throughout KID_A/Shutterstock.com; p. 5 David M. Benett/Contributor/WireImage/Getty Images; p. 7 Kevork Djansezian/Stringer/Getty Images Sport/Getty Images; p. 9 Brian Stukes/Contributor/Getty Images Entertainment/Getty Images; p. 11 JOE KLAMAR/Staff/AFP/Getty Images; p. 13 Jesse Grant/Stringer/Getty Images Entertainment/Getty Images; p. 15 Shahar Azran/Contributor/WireImage/Getty Images; p. 17 Alberto E. Rodriguez/Staff/Getty Images Entertainment/Getty Images; p. 19 Jeff Spicer/Contributor/FilmMagic/Getty Images; p. 21 Chris Polk/VMN18/Contributor/Getty Images; pp. 23, 29 Jeff Kravitz/Contributor/FilmMagic, Inc/Getty Images; p. 25 Rich Polk/Stringer/Getty Images Entertainment/Getty Images; p. 27 Steve Granitz/Contributor/WireImage/Getty Images.

Printed in the United States of America

Some of the images in this book illustrate individuals who are models. The depictions do not imply actual situations or events.

CPSIA compliance information: Batch #CW20GS: For further information contact Gareth Stevens, New York, New York at 1-800-542-2595.

CONTENTS

AN INSPIRING STORY

Chadwick Boseman is best known for bringing the first black superhero—Black Panther—to life. However, he's also played many other black heroes on the big screen. His movies, such as *Black Panther*, have **inspired** people around the world, and his life story is inspiring too!

BEHIND THE SCENES

BLACK PANTHER IS ALSO KNOWN AS T'CHALLA. HE'S THE KING OF THE **FICTIONAL** AFRICAN COUNTRY OF WAKANDA IN MARVEL MOVIES AND COMIC BOOKS.

5

GROWING UP

Chadwick Boseman was born on November 29, 1977. He grew up in the town of Anderson, South Carolina. His parents, Carolyn and Leroy, worked hard to set a good example for their three sons. Chadwick looked up to his two older brothers, Derrick and Kevin.

BEHIND THE SCENES

CHADWICK WAS A GREAT BASKETBALL PLAYER IN HIGH SCHOOL, AND HE STILL LOVES BASKETBALL. HE WENT TO A SLAM DUNK **CONTEST** IN 2018 AND LET ONE OF THE PLAYERS WEAR HIS BLACK PANTHER MASK!

TELLING STORIES

When Chadwick was in high school, a boy he played basketball with was shot and killed. Chadwick wrote a play to help him deal with his feelings. Writing the play helped him see that he wanted to tell stories when he grew up.

BEHIND THE SCENES

CHADWICK STUDIED DIRECTING AT HOWARD UNIVERSITY IN WASHINGTON, DC. HE ALSO STUDIED IN OXFORD, ENGLAND. HE WANTED TO BE A WRITER AND A DIRECTOR, BUT HE ALSO TOOK SOME ACTING CLASSES.

A MOVIE STAR

When Chadwick finished school, he acted on some TV shows. His big break came when he played the famous baseball player Jackie Robinson in the movie *42*. Jackie Robinson was the first African American to play for a **Major League Baseball** team in modern times.

BEHIND THE SCENES

CHADWICK PLAYED THE FAMOUS SINGER JAMES BROWN IN THE 2014 MOVIE *GET ON UP*. IN THE 2017 MOVIE *MARSHALL*, HE PLAYED THURGOOD MARSHALL, WHO FOUGHT FOR EQUAL RIGHTS FOR AFRICAN AMERICANS.

11

THE ONLY CHOICE

Chadwick's life changed forever in 2014 when he was cast as Black Panther. He was the only actor considered for the part, and he'd been thinking about the part for a long time. He'd even written down his own ideas for a movie about Black Panther!

STAN LEE

BEHIND THE SCENES

BLACK PANTHER FIRST APPEARED
IN COMIC BOOKS IN 1966. HE WAS
CREATED BY STAN LEE AND JACK KIRBY.
THE CHARACTER BECAME PART OF THE
GROUP OF SUPERHEROES KNOWN
AS THE AVENGERS IN 1968.

BECOMING BLACK PANTHER

Becoming Black Panther

wasn't easy! Chadwick had to

work hard and train for many

hours to play such a strong

superhero. He worked with

a special trainer to practice

martial arts, which are kinds

of fighting and self-defense

people take part in as sports.

BEHIND THE SCENES

CHADWICK WANTED T'CHALLA TO HAVE AN ACCENT, OR WAY OF SPEAKING, THAT SOUNDED LIKE PEOPLE FROM AFRICA. HE WORKED WITH A SPECIAL TEACHER TO GET IT RIGHT.

FIRST MARVEL MOVIE

Chadwick first played Black Panther in the 2016 movie *Captain America: Civil War.* In this movie, he acted with well-known Marvel actors, such as Robert Downey Jr. and Chris Evans. Chadwick fit in well. Many people said he was one of the best parts of the movie!

BEHIND THE SCENES

MANY PEOPLE WENT TO SEE THE MARVEL SUPERHEROES FIGHT EACH OTHER IN *CAPTAIN AMERICA: CIVIL WAR*. THE MOVIE MADE MORE THAN $1 BILLION IN TICKET SALES AROUND THE WORLD!

MAKING HISTORY

In 2018, Chadwick helped make history with *Black Panther*. He was the first African American actor to star in his own Marvel movie. The movie meant a lot to many African Americans because it told a powerful story about black men and women.

RYAN
COOGLER

BEHIND THE SCENES

RYAN COOGLER, THE DIRECTOR OF
BLACK PANTHER, MADE HISTORY IN HIS
OWN WAY. HE WAS THE FIRST AFRICAN
AMERICAN TO DIRECT A MARVEL MOVIE.
HE WAS ALSO THE YOUNGEST PERSON
TO DIRECT A MARVEL MOVIE.

19

BREAKING RECORDS

People loved *Black Panther*! It made more than $700 million in the United States, which was more money than any other Marvel movie had made at the time. It also made more money than any other movie in 2018.

BEHIND THE SCENES

DISNEY OWNS MARVEL STUDIOS—THE COMPANY THAT MAKES MARVEL MOVIES. IT HONORED THE SUCCESS OF *BLACK PANTHER* BY GIVING $1 MILLION TO A GROUP THAT HELPS KIDS LEARN **STEM SKILLS.**

AN AWARD WINNER

Black Panther also won many awards, or special honors. In 2019, it won the Screen Actors Guild Award for the best cast in a movie. Other actors vote for who wins this award. Chadwick gave a speech when *Black Panther* won.

BEHIND THE SCENES

THE MOST FAMOUS AWARD A MOVIE CAN WIN IS THE ACADEMY AWARD, OR OSCAR, FOR BEST PICTURE. IN 2019, *BLACK PANTHER* BECAME THE FIRST SUPERHERO MOVIE TO BE **NOMINATED** FOR THIS AWARD. HOWEVER, IT DIDN'T WIN.

JOINING THE AVENGERS

Only a few months after *Black Panther* came out, fans were able to see Chadwick in action again in *Avengers: Infinity War*. The next year, he also played Black Panther in the successful Marvel movie *Avengers: Endgame.*

BEHIND THE SCENES

MARVEL STUDIOS MOVIES, INCLUDING *BLACK PANTHER* AND THE *AVENGERS* MOVIES, ARE PART OF WHAT'S CALLED THE MARVEL CINEMATIC UNIVERSE, OR MCU. THE MCU STARTED IN 2008 WITH THE MOVIE *IRON MAN*.

MORE MOVIES

Soon after *Black Panther* came out, Marvel said it would be making a second movie about this superhero. Chadwick kept busy until then with other movies. In 2019, he starred as a **detective** in the movie *21 Bridges*.

BEHIND THE SCENES

CHADWICK ALSO KEEPS BUSY GIVING BACK TO HIS COMMUNITY. FOR EXAMPLE, HE PAID FOR MORE THAN 300 KIDS FROM HIS HOMETOWN OF ANDERSON TO SEE *BLACK PANTHER*.

A ROLE MODEL

Chadwick Boseman has starred in movies that have made a lot of money and won big awards. More importantly, though, they've given people role models, or people to look up to. By wanting to make a difference and working hard, Chadwick has become a role model too!

BEHIND THE SCENES

IN *BLACK PANTHER*, T'CHALLA AND OTHER CHARACTERS SHOW THEIR PRIDE FOR THEIR COUNTRY BY CROSSING THEIR ARMS AND SAYING "WAKANDA FOREVER!" PEOPLE AROUND THE WORLD STARTED DOING THIS AFTER SEEING THE MOVIE.

TIMELINE

1977 CHADWICK BOSEMAN IS BORN ON NOVEMBER 29.

2000 CHADWICK FINISHES SCHOOL AT HOWARD UNIVERSITY.

2013 CHADWICK STARS IN *42*.

2014 CHADWICK STARS IN *GET ON UP*.
CHADWICK IS CAST AS BLACK PANTHER.

2016 BLACK PANTHER APPEARS IN HIS FIRST MARVEL MOVIE, *CAPTAIN AMERICA: CIVIL WAR*.

2017 CHADWICK STARS IN *MARSHALL*.

2018 *BLACK PANTHER* OPENS.
MARVEL SAYS IT'S MAKING A SECOND *BLACK PANTHER* MOVIE.
AVENGERS: INFINITY WAR OPENS.

2019 *BLACK PANTHER* BECOMES THE FIRST SUPERHERO MOVIE TO BE NOMINATED FOR A BEST PICTURE OSCAR.
BLACK PANTHER WINS A SCREEN ACTORS GUILD AWARD FOR BEST CAST IN A MOVIE.
AVENGERS: ENDGAME OPENS.

FOR MORE INFORMATION

BOOKS

DiPrimio, Pete. *Chadwick Boseman*. Kennett Square, PA: Purple Toad Publishing, 2018.

Santos, Rita. *Chadwick Boseman: Superstar of Black Panther*. New York, NY: Enslow Publishing, 2018.

Zalewski, Aubrey. *Chadwick Boseman*. North Mankato, MN: Capstone Press, 2020.

WEBSITES

Disney Movies: *Black Panther*
movies.disney.com/black-panther
On Disney's website, you can learn more about *Black Panther* and download an activity packet based on the movie.

IMDb: Chadwick Boseman
www.imdb.com/name/nm1569276/
The Internet Movie Database's page on Chadwick Boseman has facts about his life and movies.

Marvel: Black Panther
www.marvel.com/characters/black-panther-t-challa
Marvel's website has the latest news and other facts about Black Panther.

GLOSSARY

contest: an event in which people try to win by doing something better than others

create: to make something

detective: a police officer whose job is to find out the facts about a crime

fictional: from a made-up story

inspire: to cause someone to want to do something great

Major League Baseball: the professional league for baseball in the United States and Canada

nominate: to suggest someone or something for an honor

STEM: a group of subjects that deal with science and math and how they're put into practice. It stands for science, technology, engineering, and math.

INDEX